DINOSAURS

BRACHIOSAURUS

by Tammy Gagne

raintree

a Capstone company — publishers for children

Raintree is an imprint of Capstone Global Library Limited, a company incorporated in England and Wales having its
registered office at 264 Banbury Road, Oxford, OX2 7DY – Registered company number: 6695582

www.raintree.co.uk
myorders@raintree.co.uk

Edited by Hank Musolf
Designed by Charmaine Whitman
Picture research by Kelly Garvin
Production by Laura Manthe
Illustrated by Jon Hughes/Capstone Press
Originated by Capstone Global Library Ltd
Printed and bound in India

ISBN 978 1 4747 5224 4
22 21 20 19 18
10 9 8 7 6 5 4 3 2 1

British Library Cataloguing in Publication Data
A full catalogue record for this book is available from the British Library.

Design elements: Shutterstock/Krasovski Dmitri

Contents

Meet the brachiosaurus

The brachiosaurus did not look like the other dinosaurs of its time. This dinosaur's front legs were longer than its back legs. Its long neck made it look a bit like a giraffe.

The brachiosaurus was about twice as tall as a giraffe. This dinosaur was more than 12 metres (40 feet) tall. The brachiosaurus weighed more than 25 tonnes.

Lots of leaves

The brachiosaurus was a herbivore. This means it survived by eating plants. It could reach leaves on top of the tallest trees.

The brachiosaurus had teeth shaped like spoons. It used them to strip the leaves from tree branches. The brachiosaurus swallowed its food whole.

Scientists think the brachiosaurus spent most of its time eating. It needed to eat 400 kilograms (880 pounds) of plants each day.

Living long ago

The brachiosaurus lived in Africa, Europe and North America. Its bones have been found in all of these places. The bones date back to 150 million years ago.

The brachiosaurus probably stayed on flat land. The brachiosaurus could feed from many trees without moving its feet. It just moved its neck.

Safety in size and numbers

Brachiosauruses travelled in herds.

These groups stayed in one

place as long as they had food.

Then they would move

to a new area.

Scientists do not think adult brachiosauruses had any predators. Older brachiosauruses protected younger ones if a bigger dinosaur came close.

Glossary

herbivore animal that only eats plants

herd large group of animals that lives or moves together

predator animal that hunts other animals for food

scientist person who studies the way the world works

Read more

Dinosaurs (Usborne Beginners), Stephanie Turnbull (Usborne Publishing Ltd, 2006)

First Facts: Dinosaurs, DK (DK Children, 2012)

World's Biggest Dinosaurs (Extreme Dinosaurs), Rupert Matthews (Raintree, 2012)

Websites

www.bbc.co.uk/cbeebies/curations/dinosaur-facts

www.dkfindout.com/uk/dinosaurs-and-prehistoric-life/dinosaurs/brachiosaurus

Comprehension questions

1. Why do you think the brachiosaurus spent so much of its time eating?

2. How do scientists know how big the brachiosaurus was?

3. Why do you think the size of the brachiosaurus stopped predators from hunting it?

Index